Understanding Coding with

SCRATCH

Patricia Harris

PowerKiDS
press

New York

Published in 2016 by The Rosen Publishing Group, Inc.
29 East 21st Street, New York, NY 10010

First Edition

Editor: Greg Roza
Book Design: Michael J. Flynn

Photo Credits: Cover © iStockphoto/mitgirl; cover, pp. 3–24 (coding background) Lukas Rs/Shutterstock.com; p. 5 Shannon Fagan/The Image Bank/Getty Images; p. 7 (girl) Blend Images/Shutterstock.com; pp. 7, 10–12, 14, 16–17, 19 (Scratch screenshots and sprites) Scratch is developed by the Lifelong Kindergarten Group at the MIT Media Lab. See http://scratch.mit.edu; p. 9 Tyler Olson/Shutterstock.com; p. 13 Alena Ozerova/Shutterstock.com; p. 15 Pornsak Paewlumfaek/Shutterstock.com; p. 17 (boy) wavebreakmedia/Shutterstock.com; p. 21 Comstock Images/Stockbyte/Getty Images.

Cataloging-in-Publication Data

Harris, Patricia.
Understanding coding with scratch / by Patricia Harris.
p. cm. — (Kids can code)
Includes index.
ISBN 978-1-5081-4482-3 (pbk.)
ISBN 978-1-5081-4483-0 (6-pack)
ISBN 978-1-5081-4484-7 (library binding)
1. Computer programming — Juvenile literature. 2. Programming languages (Electronic computers) — Juvenile literature. I. Harris, Patricia, 1949-. II. Title.
QA76.52 H37 2016
005.1—d23

Manufactured in the United States of America

CPSIA Compliance Information: Batch #BW16PK: For Further Information contact Rosen Publishing, New York, New York at 1-800-237-9932

Contents

Do It from Scratch!

Have you heard the expression "from scratch"? This means to make something using basic parts, starting at the very beginning. "Scratch" is the name of one of the most popular **computer languages**.

Scratch is based on an earlier computer language called Logo. First created in 1967, Logo has gone through a lot of changes. In the 1990s, computer scientists made Logo easier to use by employing prewritten code blocks instead of lines of code. Logo became the basis for Scratch.

The first **version** of Scratch was introduced in 2007. The Scratch creative team had kids in mind when creating the **software**. They wanted Scratch to be meaningful for users and easily shared. They also wanted to encourage kids to tinker, or experiment, with coding.

Breaking the Code

One inspiration for Scratch was a simple toy that children had been playing with for years—Lego™ building blocks! Blocks of Scratch code are made to snap together just like toy blocks.

Scratch is open-source software, which means anyone can use it for free.

Lines and Blocks

When you hear the word "coding," you might think of long pages of text and symbols. That's not the case with Scratch. Scratch eliminates the need to master **complicated** code by packaging **commands** in colorful blocks that users drag and drop into an on-screen workspace. Scratch uses different colored blocks for movements, sounds, events, and more. When users put the blocks together, they create fun figures on the screen that move and interact.

Instead of using lines of code, Scratch uses a graphical user interface, or GUI (GOO-ee). "Graphical" refers to graphics, which are pictures and shapes. "Interface" is another way to describe when two things—such as a computer and a user—communicate with each other. Scratch's GUI makes coding fun and easy!

Breaking the Code

Computer scientists developed the first GUIs in the early 1970s. Today's computers typically use GUIs to perform many tasks. Windows and Apple computer screens are GUIs that give us easy access to applications, or apps—and those apps have GUIs as well.

This is the GUI you see when you go to the Scratch website in your browser.

Follow the Rules

Before you can begin to learn about coding in any language, Scratch included, you need to know that computer programming is about following rules. Yes, that sounds a lot like playing a game, and it can be just as much fun.

Rule 1: Coders must know what they want the computer to do and write a plan.

Rule 2: Coders must use special words to have the computer take **input**, make choices, and take action.

Rule 3: Coders need to think about what tasks can be put into a group.

Rule 4: Coders need to employ **logic** using AND, OR, and NOT and other logic statements as key words.

Rule 5: Coders must explore the **environment** and understand how it works.

Computers work more efficiently if some commands are grouped, which means they can work faster.

9

Got a Plan?

Scratch is a program used to create **animations**. You choose a stage or background for the action. You choose characters called sprites. Many different sprites are included with the program. Some sprites have more than one costume, which means coders can control what the sprite looks like. You choose movements, sounds, and speech as well. You can even make your own backgrounds, sprites, and sounds.

But coders must follow the rules. You must have a plan before you begin. You must think about input, choices, and actions. You must think about grouping commands and being logical. If you want a dog to walk across the screen and bark, you need to find a dog sprite, put it on a stage, and add a bark sound. All that takes a plan.

SPRITES

STAGES

Here's a dog on a beach. The dog is a sprite, and the beach is a stage.

Scratch Blocks

Before you can begin to code with Scratch, you must understand the GUI. Here's a picture of the work screen for Scratch. On the left is a box with a cat. This is the work area for stages and sprites. The middle box is the commands area. The **scripts**, costumes, and sounds all have tabs. The different types of blocks for actions can be found by clicking on the scripts with colors beside them. The third box on the right is where the user places the blocks to build the program.

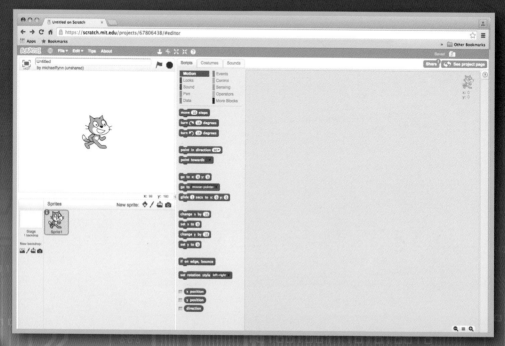

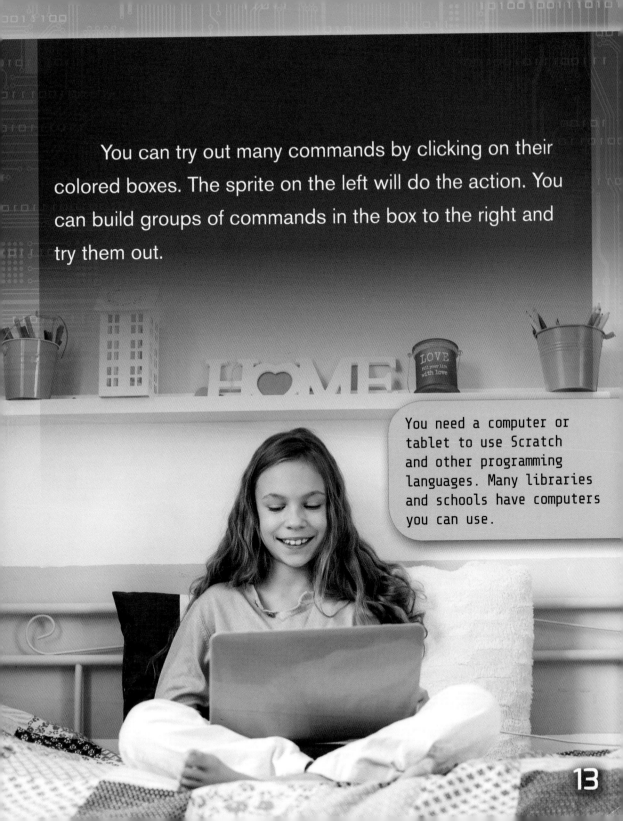

You can try out many commands by clicking on their colored boxes. The sprite on the left will do the action. You can build groups of commands in the box to the right and try them out.

You need a computer or tablet to use Scratch and other programming languages. Many libraries and schools have computers you can use.

Time to Code!

The plan for an animation with a dog can be simple. You can write: I want a dog on a beach. I want him to move his legs and walk. Here is the Scratch code for this plan.

The gold block is an Events block used to start the program. The blue Motion block has the dog in a good place to start.

A yellow Control repeat block groups tasks together. The purple Looks blocks change from one dog to another so it looks like it's moving its feet. The blue Motion blocks let the dog move. The yellow Control blocks that say "wait" are needed to slow down the computer so you can see the action.

when clicked
go to x: -151 y: -74
repeat 5
    switch costume to dog2-a ▼
    move 10 steps
    wait 1 secs
    switch costume to dog2-b ▼
    move 10 steps
    wait 1 secs

Computers work so fast that sometimes we can't see what's happening in an animation. We have to stop the action for a short time so we can see the changes being made.

15

You can add a task to your plan. You can write: I want the dog to ask if he should bark. If I say yes, he should bark. After adding this task to your plan, you now have to give the computer new lines of code. You're doing programming using input and logic.

This set of blocks lets the computer get some input. It also lets the computer decide what action to take. You let the dog ask a question. The program waits for an answer to be typed. Notice the yellow Control box that says "If." It has a logic statement in it that says if the typed answer is "yes," then the action the dog displays is a repeated bark!

```
switch costume to dog2-c ▼
ask  Do you want me to bark? Type yes or no.  and wait
wait 2 secs
think Yes or No?  for 2 secs
if      answer  = yes    then
    repeat 5
        play sound dog1 ▼
        wait 1 secs
```

Breaking the Code

Coders can copy and reuse groups of commands in a new program. That makes coding quicker.

Do you want me to bark? Type yes or no.

This is just one simple coding example. There's a lot more fun you can have with Scratch.

Put It All Together

When you want to create your own animation, here are the steps to follow:

1. **Write out a simple plan.**
   I want a sprite to move across a stage.

2. **Choose a stage and a sprite.**
   I want a dog on a beach.

3. **Think about actions you can group together so they repeat.**
   Choose a sprite with costumes. Make the costumes change and the sprite move in a repeat.

4. **Think about how to use logic in your program.**
   I want my dog to bark AND walk.

5. **Code.**

Now you're ready to try out the code and change it any way you like! You can go to the Scratch site for free. Setting up an account lets you save your work.

Want to code your own Scratch animations? Go to https://scratch.mit.edu and get coding!

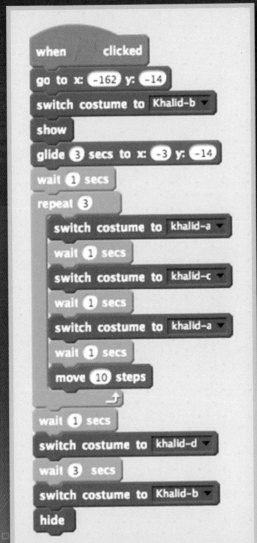

Click on the flag to start program.

Choose the starting place.

Choose the starting look.

Move smoothly to this place.

The repeat is actions you needed to group and do 3 times. You are changing the look of the sprite and taking a few steps.

You are switching to a new look.

You are hiding the sprite.

Ready to Code

Coding was once an activity for computer **designers**, software developers, and some talented hobbyists. However, Scratch is a coding program that allows inexperienced coders to see results right away. Kids as young as eight years old are using Scratch to learn about coding and have fun at the same time. Parents and teachers are also using Scratch to teach kids about coding. Even adults like to code with Scratch!

Scratch is just one program that new coders can use to learn about coding. The other books in this set offer other opportunities for you to explore coding. Now you're ready to get out there and scratch the surface of coding!

Breaking the Code

Scratch is maintained by the Lifelong Kindergarten Group located in the Massachusetts Institute of Technology (MIT) Media Lab in Cambridge, Massachusetts.

Have you learned about computer languages and coding in school? Many schools are starting to teach coding to young students.

Scratch Coding Terms

Control block—A yellow block that controls scripts, or stacks of connected blocks.

costume—A different look for a sprite. Can be used to make the sprite look like it's moving.

Events block—A gold block that decides what events occur in an animation.

Looks block—A purple block that controls a sprite's appearance.

Motion block—A blue block that tells how and where the sprite should move.

Sounds block—A light purple block used to control sounds.

sprite—A small figure or character that users animate.

stage—The background for an animation.

Glossary

animation: A movie made from a series of drawings, photographs, or computer graphics that creates the appearance of motion by small progressive changes in each image.

command: A code or message that tells a computer to do something.

complicated: Difficult to explain or understand.

computer language: A programming language designed to give instructions to a computer.

designer: Someone who plans and creates new products.

environment: The combination of computer hardware and software that allows a user to perform various tasks.

input: Information that is entered into a computer.

logic: A proper or reasonable way of thinking about or understanding something.

script: A sequence of instructions carried out by a computer program.

software: A program that runs on a computer and performs certain tasks.

version: A form of something that is different from the ones that came before it.

Index

Websites

Due to the changing nature of Internet links, PowerKids Press has developed an online list of websites related to the subject of this book. This site is updated regularly. Please use this link to access the list: www.powerkidslinks.com/kcc/scra